BLOOD HYPHEN

BLOOD HYPHEN

Kenny Williams

Oberlin College Press
Oberlin, Ohio

The FIELD Poetry Series, vol. 36
Oberlin College Press, 50 N. Professor Street, Oberlin, OH 44074
www.oberlin.edu/ocpress

Book design: Steve Farkas
Cover design: Kenny Williams and Steve Farkas
Cover image: Detail from Yolande Delasser, *Adam and Eve* (watercolor, c.
1939). Index of American Design, 1943.8.8096. Courtesy National Gallery
of Art, Washington.

Library of Congress Cataloging-in-Publication Data

Names: Williams, Kenny, 1975-
Title: Blood hyphen / Kenny Williams.
Description: Oberlin, Ohio : Oberlin College Press, 2016. | Series: The
    FIELD Poetry Series ; vol. 36
Identifiers: LCCN 2015036954| ISBN 9780932440549 (pbk. : alk. paper) |
    ISBN 0932440541 (pbk. : alk. paper)
Classification: LCC PS3623.I558325 A6 2016 | DDC 811/.6—dc23
LC record available at http://lccn.loc.gov/2015036954

For those whose blood confesses

Contents

"How shall I slumber and where shall I sleep so long as I tremble for the vine, my mother? O mother, thou art my right hand, but my left is lame, and I cannot lift it up." I cried, "My father, my father, my left hand! Half of my seed is spoilt. I am half born and half dead, always one part of two, though never two in one, the father and the mother."

Edward Dahlberg, *Because I Was Flesh*

About the Author

The genius of Diogenes:
all his books are lost.
But really that's the genius
of the books and not the man.
If I can speak for the man,
his diet of worms and onions
makes me feel like a pig
when I go to the store
and it's midnight
and the store is closing.
But in the land of the living
midnight means nothing
and the closing of the store even less.
I open the freezer and stick my head in
and taste in that strange air
both cold ends of the earth at once:
the puke-sweet honey of a wintry spring,
the stink of my weakness
for the luxury of proper action.
At home in the morning I find myself
stacking old ax handles into a pyre
for my chickens, all called Margaret,
and their sire, Mr. Margaret,
torn to shreds in their defense,
the musk of the vixen
lingering more like violets
than the season should allow.

At the Pyramids

And where have *you* been living?
(This is our neighbor at breakfast talking.)
Define living, we say.
Inhabiting? Peopling? Breakfasting?
Loving? Being married? Marrying?
Being loved? Surviving
the sucking daytime heat?
And what *was* the horse's big idea,
swimming up and bumping
our stunned and silent barge,
his buttocks slicked with mud?
Remember that girl back in Richmond,
scared out of her mind, in the open carriage
blocking traffic, her diaphanous veils
streaming after…?
Half of Broad Street wanted to stomp them,
to drag the woman down
through the purifying shit
and haul her up again,
streaked with hair and tears.
Where did she slink off to after that?
Where *are* the houses of the living?
Go and look for them now.

Capsule

So the jazzman died living in a box
and his music just left
the solar system
with *Moby Dick*
and baseball stats,
Adam and Eve abstracted
beyond recognition.
And on earth
things are as ever:
a man and a woman
go for a drive.
The night is warm.
A bird blows in.
They crash, climb free
of all that's upside down,
unbruised and sober
and going to make
serious love, having come
at last to the beginning
of their story.

The Infant

As a teacher of mine once said,
If you think I'm hard to work with
you should try *being* me.
And since I hated my teacher
and Paul in equal measure,
I tried being Paul, for the hell of it, really,
first as the saint, who taught the man
how to sin, then as the man,
the faithful teacher of the saint,
and when those got me nowhere
as the infant Paul had been,
squirming in the dust of the road,
the glorious rump of his horse
flying over him, falling away.

Alive and Dead

for Sadie Williams

St. George thought he, as in him*self*, was dead.
Not that he *had* died or maybe even *might*.
Even his horse was playing dead, almost
convinced of the fact. A bird knew better
and pecked an orange growing over their heads.
A bright drop fell into the mouth of the knight
and he got up clanking and picked the bleeding sun
and gave it to his horse to chew, and they were off
along the pre-dawn road, at the end of which
were big hot meals, and along which fresh adventures.
As a kid I was loved just enough to take the set-up
for the plot, the arrest of action for movement
if not change, in its plastic frame
tacked up in my grandmother's pantry,
among the canning of the last ten years
of her widowhood's forty,
jars of damson plums stratified like rock,
green beans faded to the green of camouflage,
their disguise wicked straight
from the rarely broken dark, and I, I think,
smugly rooting for the dragon
left behind, galloped *down*, like the road,
and the day in that frame that never broke,
with no occasion to refuse
since never offered the drop
of quick and bracing light.

The Courtship

My husband has a passion
for telling me his dreams.
This morning's was of a bellhop
in an old hotel, having his way
with a ship's pretty figurehead,
squirming against its blonde wood
like a drop of overeager blood.
It was *my* first love, he murmured,
making me a baby in his arms.
I never woke to see the daybreak's
troubled gray, but could hear the chainsaws
at work in the distance,
where the forests were content
to devour themselves
and the little red cap
to press them.

The Creature in Mourning for Its Mate

From whom has not that rude hand rent some dear connection?
Mary Shelley, *Frankenstein*

Lester, the tenant farmer's son,
has taken to dressing in nothing but the coat
he found by our hearth, steaming and half-frozen,
long and worked with gold.

He steals my razor, shaves half his head in celebration.
Man, he says, considering the captain whose coat
he thinks he wears, is wise enough
to map the seas he's daft enough to sail.

The pig we helped him fatten all through autumn,
collapses now, unbutchered,
starved less to death than dying to arouse
young Lester's interest.

His love for England's meat is for Marie.
Tackling her by the haunches, above
the bluff of chalk and liquid sea, he forces her
black face against his white, pulling it on
like a mask, swapping his look of excitement
for hers of surprise.

When, some day, your memory's lost
in all its patchwork moods, only Lady,
of our chickens, will eye me with suspicion
from her basket of eggs.

Nature Theory

With winter and daylight coming on together
I'm leading the women of the world to the woods
and splash my light across the trail map
like a signpost at the woods, made of metal
or whatever's woods-proof and hard.

I point with my stick to the point beyond which
I will not venture in the acorn-crunching dark,
and the women of the world disappear
down the path, into the woods, in Indian file
without me, who has spent his night

in their good care, needing a woman
or every one of them the world can spare,
the last one saying she grew up around here,
she knows the paths pretty well, thanks anyway,
and good luck getting back before dawn.

Enter Lilith, in Her Garden

Hammers,
I give you his hands.
Hard pavement his skull,
that he may test his ambitions
in the open air.
His heart I bequeath to you,
mothers of daughters everywhere.
His last breath to TV,
a soundbite for the ages
condensed to a drop
in a chilled silver spoon.
A perfect copy of his dick,
a field mouse cast in plaster,
since he has no grieving mother,
I bequeath to the acre
of red earth from which
the original was formed.
To his concubines,
all state-appointed,
I give his houses, one to each.
However many of you there are
that's how many houses.
And to you, strange woman
in my citrus garden, crushing
blossoms to your throat
and laughing, whose sin
was not the first, as has been
said so many times, but who
perfected it, made sin Sin,
I leave his battle scars.
His skin I leave to the rope
that burned it,

his milktooth to the thread of spit
from which it hangs.
His eyes can go
to the snake in Eden,
its point-of-view
the mere distinction
between seeing
and being seen, etc.
His doctors can have
the secret mushrooms
of his cancers,
the hot public slime
of his colostomy bags.
The drinking glass can keep
his unbreakable teeth.
To his sons of clay
I give his Memoir of Creation.
And to his bastards, you countless
sons of breath, his history
of the world in seven volumes,
forthcoming, from which
I have carefully deleted my name.
What love I had for him
I leave to Paradise,
where he was king,
or so his counselors,
that stock of furry mammals,
called him, splitting hairs
between heresies.

Memoir of Creation

I'll be the first to say it: *Light.*
I'll be the first: *That's power.*
Electricity is pure information.
I didn't say *that.*
Marshall McLuhan did
and he is the happiest of alarmists,
buried under a playground in Thornhill, Ontario.

The snow goose, with his black wings,
acknowledges the light of Light,
but that's cheating.
Jellyfish do it too,
like there's no tomorrow.

The light in Florida does it,
though it's never carried a palm
swaying through my eye,
which is to say I've never seen a palm
in person, but have it on Chesterton's authority:
the palm's a masterpiece, quite beyond
the reach of dubitation.

Jesus' tomb flooded with light
when the door lifted off, light
as a door a third its size, the sun
rushing in to investigate,
sniffing every corner like a suspicious dog.

In innocence I bit
into the electric apple
of a Christmas ball,
the widow Sadie Williams

(always the only sober head in the room)
lifting the shards from my mouth
with raw dough.
It was a beginning of being loved
but not an end
to my taste for orbs and eyeballs,
models of the world
in white chocolate, broken
strings of pearl.

I could probably go forever
without seeing another snow goose erection,
without plucking the planets
from the seething dark
like chestnuts from the fire.

There's a picture you should know:
Georges de la Tour, *Job Mocked by His Bride*.
See how she's lit from inside, like a lamp.

Or just drive down the street any Christmas
before noon, and count the porch lights,
dim bulbs still thinking
it's the night before.

Sugar Blues

Park & Stuart Aves., Richmond

The streetlamps are black, the gutter
stitching itself into a skin
of ice.

A man drags a tree down the street
toward the park,
shouting Christmas songs and the praises
of beautiful lights.

The imperishable minuteman holds forth
his gun,
looks out in heartbreak at the city
in its sleep,
under its flashing plastic star.

The man with the tree
whips the doll from the manger,
plants his tree *in* the manger, shouting now
at the manger
for comfort and joy.

Neighbor, cool your anger.
Ours is a wandering, homeless race
and the manger is our grave
standing ready, the sweetest
powder on its lips.

Tough Room

The night of the fancy dress ball
the fancy dress ball never happened.
I sat on the porch in my feathers and furs,
sipping sherry and watching the snow
become impassible.

The stoplight pulsed at the end of the lane,
and I could feel the sherry inside me, pulsing.

Had I an audience I'd compare myself to Donne
preaching to the quality, his bitterest critics
snoozing in the pews, wrapped warm in horsehair
right under his nose.

The simpler the statement of fact,
the poet found, the more objectionable,
unutterable even to himself,
the crickets of summer his only advocates,
sleeping their deaths off like hangovers
under the "blackness of snow."

I say *blackness of snow* because
the Muses never knew me.
Art got smart and the Muses got heckled
right out of the West, like Old West bandits,
their left boots bleeding, the bank half-robbed.

When you're telling the truth
there's always something left to say
about the torments of hot and cold,
how they ride into town
masquerading as weather.

Palace of Illusion

for Rusty Levenson

I take a sledge to the bust of Berkeley,
a box cutter to half a dozen portraits
of empiricists in important wigs.
I open a water main and wash away
the treasures of ancient Japan.
I pull all the fake Franz Klines off the wall.
The real ones are hiding behind them.
These I set on fire but the fakes are so good
the flames jump indifferently between,
hopelessly in love with either.
I touch my lighter to some mohair braids
and the Rare Dolls Room goes up
like a foundling home in a Russian photo.
Now the lighter's a bat. Those stupid eggs explode
in a universe of pink and purple stars.
I shoot the picture of Lincoln, pistol-whip
the unresisting Buddha, kick a Boucher
in the ass, my boots crunching over breadcrumbs
of marble and through splinters of gilded frame.
But I pause at an Annunciation, the usual girl
and angel, the lily in a vase, the dove
in hesitation. Plus a couple of buntings
in a silver cage, some chickens looking ruffled
and incensed, just run from the barn to the house
through the worst hailstorm in memory.
I let my ax go limp, banish from my mind
the rise and fall of Rome, the room-filling
abstractions just begging to be bombed.
I stoop and start sweeping the floor
with my hands. I build a little pyramid
of soot, the feast of an ash-fed flower.
I do not wonder that God's messenger
should cluck at what I do, that the lily
should nod in my direction.

Bled to the Edges

for David

All night you make your rounds in the Museum.
As I'm crawling into our huge bed
I see you step before the *Adoration,*
and in your uniform of blue and black
you start to cry—not big tears
like you sometimes see men try to hide
in the prime of handsome middle age,
when it hits them that we are not men
without our bodies, more by ourselves
than with any other. Tonight, in bed,
by the rack your uniform goes to
to be alone, I crawl back into mine.
I want for yours and you for the Lord's
laid low among the beasts that understand it.

The Hurricane

after letters from William Maxwell to Sylvia Townsend Warner

The neighbor phoned and said our apple trees,
a hundred years old and very beautiful, were gone,
but he is the happiest of alarmists.
One crashed into his Chevrolet, with Poilu,
his poodle, inside, who savaged the upholstery.
For six days there were no lights
(one of your favorite themes)
and sometimes nothing to cook on.
But our orchard wasn't gone, but changed.
Where it had been a double alley of complex trees
now it was a simple and random delight.
You couldn't tell by the shards
what had perished.

On the Feast Day of the Beheading of St. John the Baptist

August 29, 2010

Emptying the fridge by candlelight.
Jellies drop into a flimsy bag.
They might have gone
ages ago, the fancy marmalades,
their clouds of white hair
rounding out to crowns,
taking the shape of their jars.
And these two plums,
bearded and wise, reared half a year
under a thousand panes of glass,
from seeds like nuggets of mahogany...
a couple of philosophers
who spent their best years writing
long long letters to each other
from opposite corners
of their madhouse room.
Which Hume were they arguing about
when they agreed
the tongue is totally desperate
and irreclaimable?
In its cold confinement each insists
on *its* Hume,
while the candle flame's
obnoxious witness asks
only that their flesh be given
to the trash, their temptations
to the black and balmy winds.

Lincoln in the Holy Land

for Verlon Vrana

There's no getting past it:
the actor's pellet whispered its
hot word right past his ear.
There were *two* carriages,
another time.
He took the one that wasn't
what exploded.
He was robbed of death
a dozen novel ways,
he didn't like to think
by Providence, or even Fate,
given a term no more certain
than the assassin's.
To Bethlehem, on horseback, then,
the old man squinted
on scrubby hills.
The landscape rippled
while the world stayed flat.
There was a parable he made up
as he went:
The Parable of the Hayseed,
the papers called it, then complained
it was too dense
and, for once, like the mule,
too short.
His voice I do not dare speak in.
I even shudder
pulling on his suit
of bones.
I am but the stork of myth,

folding every awkward angle
through the door of the Church
of the Nativity, a mere porthole
and the only way inside.
And even here,
our Republic's private citizen,
he's handed telegraphed appeals:
"This man, Mr. Lincoln,
must not be executed."

Simon of Cyrene

Every eye that looks on God
can look on you,
and you can live.
You won't burn up
or vanish into nothing.
When it's done
you can limp back
to your borrowed house,
curse the name of the city,
complain to your wife,
have her wash the blood
from your clothes
and rub your screaming back
and clean your cuts.
And in the night
perturbed by men and animals,
you can wake beside her
who's climbing over you
toward your screaming sons,
and who will, in her time,
climb back, like all good things
too good to be believed.

Samuel Butler

If I had been born in the time of Christ, I trust I should not have been among his disciples. I hope I might have been among those who crucified him.

Samuel Butler, notebook entry

Your life's work done,
it's time to ease the nails out, Sam,
like straight pins, by the rainbow
beads of their heads.

The nail holes grow as they close
against your lips, your mouth
more wet than scarlet,
new-hatched anguish in its nest of fur.

It's not the nails
your tongue and mind agree on,
it's the boards, the vacant X,
Christ's feet and hands four wandering flags
forsaken by the pole.

Feel without Him how easy
the wobbly world is righted,
with what a cry of bliss
the long-dead boards break themselves
back into the tree.

For a lover like you,
the boards would give anything
to grow again, even their lives, and do.

Sorry to Ask

Sorry to ask, but was it funny or sad
that the swan fell in love with a paddleboat?
That the dancer took a thousand leaps
before he took the one that stunned the world?
That the voicemail started out *It's me, just me,*
and after that was just words in a voice
you'd never heard before? You know as well as I do
the swan can't go on, nursing his first crush forever.
The dancer can't leap without end in endless space.
And the checking of that mail, whether it's two seconds
or a thousand years from now, that voice you don't know
calling all the dead by their proper names?
It's the same as when you catch up with a friend
at a bar, after "it's been too long," and she looks
hard at the ring of water between her hands
flat on the table, and she says, *Well...*

Concrete Poem

for Peter Kreeft

I was a writer in another life. Now I am God.
At night I light the lawns for miles around
with my door whose door has become a writing table
with four stout legs screwed on.
The concrete populations of lawn and garden
gather toward me, doorstops for my door of light.
And even in that crowd, where any concrete persons
could disappear, the saint and the gnome stand out
together, as obvious as a couple of secret lovers,
each guarding the other from the only
Virgin in the neighborhood
endowed at birth with concrete clothes.

Not on the Lips

I read all about St.-Michel, the church
that floats above the tidal plain, but never went
to worship there. Henry Adams went to see it
and says he fell in love, and that makes it dangerous.
J. A. Baker—he loved everything there is to love
about the hawk. He might have been the greatest
lover ever, but I'll never know. I'll never read him.
Where could I be that the church won't soar, the hawk
refuse to stoop? I was born a solipsist, for sure,
but died a lapwing, looking for grub
at the bottom of the unsuspecting sky.

Up and Over

I hover just over
the clay like God.
I hover just over
the clay like a lover,
spread myself
across the ground
we're hardly part of
anymore.

I'm dying to peel
my powdered wig off.
The morning's
so desperately hot.
But I want so bad
to *stay* like Newton,
who died a virgin,
probably, or even
like Descartes,
who pushed the love
and clay apart.

In the end I want
to thank the Lord
for the common sense
of copper pots
and indestructible skillets
that admit to themselves
they will never be God,
that the blue sizzling power
really never was theirs.

Blood Hyphen

The mother's here
to peel the sheet back
from the feet,
the broken legs,
the battered groin,
the sex engorged,
wreathed around the base
with bruises and thorns
tattooed in convolution.
She'd gasped a little
at his first erection, too,
what she thought *must* be,
that leveling stiffness
as she held him, eight days old
and receiving his name,
the prepuce pinched away:
a delicate specimen,
almost botanical.
In Heaven, she guessed,
where all half-measures fail,
you either miss it altogether
or see nothing else.
And down here, too literally
underground, her son's gut plundered
for procedure's sake and quickly
closed, she finds the blood
like a black silk scarf
pulled endlessly, at leisure,
from a not-quite-open drawer,
slipped around his cock in play,
the last wound used to rouse the first.

Work and Word

"Don't you know that we shall judge the angels?"
Paul, First Corinthians

When every word,
every work of the hand
is assessed, forgiven,
discarded and made known,
the angels will snap to attention
before us, in admiration
and embarrassment,
barely able to resist
the urge to wiggle the nubs
of their amputated wings.
And you swore we'd never
be so beautiful again!

Clear and Copious

Don't talk to me
about Schumann bereft of reason,
but in the moment just before.
Don't talk to me about the life
of the biographer
who spent more time
with Schumann than Schumann,
or of the life of the biographer's son
and heir to nothing,
a locksmith balancing a pick on his nose,
his life's ambition to make it stand
until his girlfriend sees.
And for God's sake don't speculate
it wasn't the lunatic that wrote the song
so utterly forgettable
the biographer himself wouldn't know it
if he heard it whistled halfway
down the road.

Applause

You got here late, just as I was dying.
Whatever the angels live for
the very air is humming with it here
and every hand that struck its mate
plays dead in every lap
at your appearance in the door.

Read Me All the Books

Read me all the books
by Anonymous.

Bring me all the head
of Frank Lloyd Wright.

Straighten the doornail.

Stem the rose.

Be my very flower
of discretion.

School of Practical Dissection

In the hands of the priest
the heart has to break
like crockery, for a single man,
not the human race,
which we love into oblivion
and despise in general.
In the hands of the anatomist
it leaps, the heart, like a trout—
small, brown, and poached—
at the end of the line.
Faster students than our teachers,
we feel like boys playing hooky,
just wetting our toes
in the landlord's river,
passing his jug from
mouth to mouth.

In Pleading

"and you shall be as gods"
Gen. 3:5

We are not like the animals.
Even when they scream
they keep close in themselves
the menace of eternal
silent things.
Their whole body
is their face.
When they do speak
they are nowhere all at once.
When God says Where are you?
they answer We are here
at the starting line, Lord,
before You, without dread.
We are nothing like the gods.
Their speech is thick with pictures
of themselves.
When they say God
they really mean God.
Their face at the top of them
is always a surprise.

In Boyce

Boyce is the town
with the quietest name.
It has an old stone house in it
with a bronze centaur
with a clock in its side
and a guy on the roof,
traipsing the roof, expertly
imitating the whistle
of a bird never seen
in Boyce but stuffed. There's a death-
defying moment
you catch your breath
in this world, afraid your
fellow man will lose
his whistle with his stride,
tripping from cornice
to cornice, catching himself
just in time each time.

There's a Whale Aground at Wijk aan Zee

You hate the world.
I am a planet.
You wreck the image.
I'm a picture.
You condemn the body.
I am God's bathtub
turned inside out.
I wear my ring
of residue and brine
like a girdle
at my waterline.
And what a joke,
your House of Nassau
in his ostrich-feathered hat,
scrambling down toward me
from the dunes,
a posy to his nose
lest I prove some sickening ingenuity
of Spain's.
His daughter,
following like a dog,
lifts her skirts
with astonishing ease
at sight of me, to the waist.
Squats and excitedly pees
in the sand.
So there can be
no doubt: the velvet
of her skirts is black.
Her hair is stacked
into a harness of pearls.

There's a Rooster Aboard the Battleship

Never mind what you've been told.
I never wanted to be God
but only lost together with him
in that mystery that's the Sun.
Still, I am its brother
here on earth, where *I* am king,
my crown a blood blister,
the Milky Way a frozen spark
twinkling in the nailhead
of my one good eye.
My cock-a-doodle-doo
brings forth every atom
of this black sea,
makes red the essence of light
and heavy things,
mosquito nets and 12-inch guns,
the coldness of dress whites
thrown on in wee hours,
hooch bottles capsized, like lifeboats
cooling their spanked-red bottoms
in the glow of the paschal moon.
The captain of this boat and you
make such an ugly a couple,
he so old and you so young,
he so harsh and you so tender.
Look past him, then, and through
the mounted telescope's single
bloodshot eye, your Dixie cup hat
in your trembling hands.
Fill your head with undrinkable
horizon, the solitude-tormented beast
of the Sun I holler forth

just now as it peaks the water's rim,
and thank your earthly mom and pop
for putting you in a sailor suit
and putting you out to sea.
An astrologer had told them
you should die by water,
and here you are, in my little boat,
dying of nothing.
Scanning the winking sea.
A telescope, on another boat,
winking at you through yours.

Rosemary Lamb

The heaven of the gods that are not God
is never big enough. It's always filling up
with smoke, the greasy breath
of sacrifice, which gods alone can take as food.
Our Father gave this business up
to stink up our bright booths
of plush and gold. The server serves
the slaughtered lamb, the lungs
the expanding sky. I sing while I can.
The palace of the gods is always adding on.
And if you glut yourself on smoke
you'll live forever and forever
is an end to the story of the gods,
the start of all that's come before,
sheer prologue to the puff.

The Lesser Gods of Earth

Too late for the worms,
too early for the birds,
we jump like fleas
a thousand times our height,
freighted with the blood of dogs
so big you could put
saddles on them and ride,
force the frontiers back
of every hostile yard.

The Minotaur

for Clare Rossini

When Minos first saw me
he recognized, with satisfaction,
the work of bull-stupid queens,
the horrors delivered
in strange ways to kings.

With a simple lifting of his hand
he summoned the clown from Pediatrics.
He thought the rainbow-colored fool could use
an eyeful of something ugly and embarrassing,
white set next to red, not a shade of pink
in sight: a birthing room

wrecked, the woman inside
having given the gods the perfect
chance to kill her when she knew
damn well they wouldn't.

And afterwards, and just before,
she clung so hard to the midwife
she could taste her blood and mine
mingled in the old woman's hair,
could smell the wine on her breath
when she upset the bowl of poppy pods
over my steaming, royal head.

The clown, for his part,
joked that he and not the bull
might be my father, coming to the queen
under the midwife's drunken gaze.

I'm afraid the clown's world *was*
a little marvelous,
the midwife a bit too red in the nose,
the queen dragged free
of me, the breech x-rayed to show
my neck where it breaks
where the midwife breaks it.

The Tortoise

for Sarah Talbutt

The awful god of the underworld
is mourning
the absence of his wife.

When she's around you'd think
she's his daughter,
she's that awful too.

The god pulls loose his helmet
of bone,
sets it roaming over
the upper world, that it, at least,
might catch the sun on its back,
trundle like an army
through the shadows of linen
flapping over lawns.

To cross its path
is surely some kind of blessing.
You don't have to pass
the season weeping
over hairpins, makeup,
a million kinds of jewels…

Rings emptied of her fingers,
chokers of her throat.

The Hummingbird

Before they gave a concert
the Greeks would drop copper pots
on marble floors,
so you could hear the silence
reassembling itself, a blank space
for the flute.
More like what we'd call a kazoo.
And what's with the hummingbird
planted in the mouth?
My mother used to fill a feeder
with sugar and water
and turn up her crooked but decidedly
feminine thumbs.
"The ones that come are *this big*,"
she would say, for those of us
that won't rest without removing
our mothers' hands
with precision saws, who want to scream
but are afraid of shattering that silence
in which we'll have to hand
their old hands back to them,
priceless pairs of antique cups
they want to drink from
but can only drop.

The Raccoon

for Bill Norris, my grandfather

She steps into the old
mill stream, a slip
of charcoal fur
like a petal of sugar,
plucked from a sugar rose,
held in her sharp teeth.
Her head dips under
the cold bright stream,
her muzzle raised above it.
Her egg-bred skin of lice and fleas
that calls her food and home
mobs the sleek length,
the whole province
of her body, to the highest
ground, the tag of fur
above the flood.
It must feel good,
bringing all that death
into the world
the way she does,
or rather just letting it go.

Pearls Before Swine

It's the kind of place people say
"Let's scramble up to the obelisk
before we dress for dinner"
and mean it literally: there's an obelisk
at the top of the hill, just for fun.

The heir apparent is assumed
blown to pieces in the field
but he's here on the breastworks
in his snappy uniform, straightening
his back against the photographer's
carefully chosen stormclouds.

Below them, in the dust,
I'm eating my soup out of a helmet.

When I was the boy's age I almost choked
laughing: the Monseigneur had told us
a story around his smoky table,
but now it's going to rain and wash out
the last little dryness of its joke.

At the station the boy will send
some lady's maid or shell-deafened gardener
before him, to break the news of his living
and being almost home.

The story that almost killed me
ended with a cardinal's mistress walking
her pig on a leash—a drop on my bald spot—
through the streets of Rome.

Filler Material

In Tucson there is a lab
expressly dedicated to extracting
sunlight from pears,
which costs the pears their lives.
And still I envy them.
To have ears is to listen in terror
as the newsman gets it wrong.
Tolstoy did not say
all happy endings are alike!
From an infinity of possible beginnings
Tolstoy was born Tolstoy
and no one else, a man of genius
living a sumptuous peasant life.
The thing to know is that his daughter
gave birth before she made it through
the orchard to the house.
It was only March, the orchard
already blooming pear
and the great man in his summer hut,
dressed as a Caucasian mountaineer,
just adjusting his impeccable scarlet hose,
didn't hear her screaming
any more than the sun did,
spilling down her open throat.
Mother, child and Count
lived well long after that, of course,
but for this the newsman has no use.
In times way worse than these
pears were ornamental, plentiful
and nothing you could chew.

The House with Two Front Doors

Tolstoy would leave notes for his wife
in his diary, small instructions
and requests, flirting
admonitions—

My Queen, my bee,
my sovereign of wax and honey,
of sweetness and of light,
for whom my praise of everything
has been but sorry preparation
for my praising you,
what you've burned in candles this month
the rest of us could work by
for a year!—

and joking hints of other
notes in other diaries, almost
of other wives, likewise
intended for Sophie's looking for
but never for her finding.

Operation Daily Bread

Nevada Test Site, 1953

There will be a fire
that blocks out the sun.
For now, though,
in the four—give it five—
long seconds before,
there's a dinner being eaten
in the middle of the day.
Good thing we're not robbers.
The crystal's cheap.
There's nothing in it.
No sharp white wine,
no day-old fish.
The blazer hangs a little loosely
on the host.
But where's our hostess,
the plastic lady
in the brand new dress,
a clean and simple thing,
very dark blue, with a fine
white dot in the print?
The windows are all open.
Did the hostess get away?
The desert air takes the wind
with it when it leaves.
How many seconds have we got,
counting backward?
Three? More likely two.
Just time enough to beg
our daily bread, but can we
receive it in good faith,

now, having broken—
looking for it—in?
The dead calm face
of the host says, *Go.*
Come ask again tomorrow,
by which the dead calm
face means, as it's melting,
you should have come
asking yesterday.

Robert Frost Embarks on Goodwill Tour of Soviet Republics

Maya Plisetskaya, Queen of Swans,
was on her way out for the People's Meeting
when Hermes, the houseboy, announced
there was a man, and there he was, her Uncle Sam
of shaggy, lowered brow, on her horsehair sofa,
irretrievably drunk. How you *live*, she said.
He was back from the dead, he said, to take it up again,
the old courtship. The dropped string.
His breath when she kissed him was odious—
the sour weather blowing always through his words.
A right and true crafts man! she'd tell the auditorium,
in some kind of abstract awe, but never *poet*.
She said it that way, *crafts* (one word), *man* (another)
on its heels. Three months they would live, crafts
man and Queen, the length of a New England season,
in her Petersburg flat, making rigorous love
and listening to the neighbors downstairs
beat the hell out of each other, until the State slipped in
and put things right where fists could only fail.
The ruckus they took when they were disappeared
made him think of a horse on its side,
trying to stand among tables and chairs.
People—when they're problems—come in pairs.
She laughed like a horse when he said that
and he fell right out of love, three months
of hating the tulle she wore, the horse
in the mousehole, the swans in her heart
that fed on grubs, what was left of his wife's
lettuce patch, savaged back home and after rain.
The People, yes!—a moment's hesitation
and his lover did most buoyantly agree.

Ars Apologia

for Helena Wetsel

If you wait long enough
the most feared and hated
of your enemies will slip
under a pall of sympathetic love.
Whole galaxies will hatch
before your eyes,
like jellyfish dropping
through bottomless water.
After the Flood
you'll drive three miles
to see *King John* in the drizzle,
the audience hot and miserable
under its umbrellas,
the cast saying afterward
it was their best performance yet.
What else can I tell you?
I sat up half the night once,
with a flesh-and-blood woman
in the Charles City Jail,
listening with her
to the sobbing down the hall
of what she told me
only later was her ghost.

My Hero

Storming away from her mother in the market.
Get your ass back here or there'll be no ice cream.
The aisle, my favorite, Coffee and Cereals,
might as well be a country road, the runaway
glancing back over a narrow shoulder bone,
her house burning up, her bedroom
window belching animal and humanoid toys
panicked into action, falling upward in despair.
The kid raises her fists in foregone triumph,
not even near the finish line: *I'm going away for-*ever!
If you can believe her face the woman's love
is like the house, burning hotter and hotter
the farther from it you move.

House on Fire: McLean, Virginia

after Joel Sternfeld

Legend will have it
this fire was staged,
the mess of pumpkins
carefully arranged
on the brown grass,
the fireman posed
with a big one
couched in his rescuing arm
as he searches the stand
across the road from the house
for another perfect pumpkin
to match: an identical twin
from rows and rows
of ugly, unexploded cousins.

But the ladder trucks *have* rushed
into the scene, lie concealed almost
completely, behind some privet hedge
and threadbare crepe that wasn't
planted sixty years ago for you
not to look for the ladder trucks through.

The biggest truck extends a bucket
toward the house's roof of flame.
The roof pulls away, just smudging
the ceiling of unfallen snow.

I've searched my soul and can't, in words,
make real my hatred of this poem, forced
here in the open to face itself as less
than it would hope to be: the house
I build to burn.

Drop your eye from the roof, then,
to the pumpkins on the grass,
blazing orange to orange, and see
how the man carries on,
calmly browsing pumpkins
at the roadside stand, shirking
the work the poet won't.

The Caravan

The caravan unloads,
the cages unlock,
a penknife is produced
to trim a wick.
The pinhead knows
the world isn't flat
but hasn't known enough
not to lose her candle stump.
The wedding party
of her friends,
the Bearded Lady
and the Bearded Lord,
rides over the mud
on duckboards,
and the two-headed girl
(the one bridesmaid)
can't stop laughing!
She's never seen a horse
composed of two people,
the push and pull
of ass and head.
As for the celebrated
mesmerist, he hops on
and rides off in all directions.

Soak the Bloke

The naked clown, pitching his tent
outside the fairgrounds,
might as well be any hairy ape
without his rainbow skin.
All day he catcalls women,
teases children, curses men
from his perch above a tank
of rainbow-tinted water.
Ball after ball is bought
and thrown, and he's in,
pressing a red rubber nose
to the porthole, pulling
what he hopes are terrifying
unforgettable faces.
The women relax into laughter.
The men turn away,
a little disgusted,
but laughing, too.
The kids see other kids
crying without trying to,
their sad balloons round again
and rising, and ask their parents,
in the public toilet or the car,
if it's the clown that is the reason
for the fair...
asking, without meaning to,
if it's really *God*
that made the world,
the answer just that laughter
only those known
deeply for themselves
can ever speak of after.

Note on Spurious Sources

Hell was a fair place. The water of the lake was blue.
Olive Schreiner

The lake opened between Alps
like a sudden eye. The eye was blue,
which you don't need me to tell you.
I have to say it for myself,
just as I have to tell you I had to
hear all the great requiems
in a single summer day,
starting after breakfast
and going way past dark,
all that grief and majesty
belching out the window
while I lounged in wicker
between the stumpy blues of Virginia.
All that morning the chaise was white,
but this goes without saying.
The fence was white and the dogs
half-asleep at my feet,
the sky blank and dull,
staved with old phone lines.
I wonder about the angels,
if they go around in Hell
with looks of indignation,
because they are deathless
and understand at last
not who but *what* they are,
and never cry aloud in praise
of what there's no word for
except for *Home.*

Fixing *Miss Becky*'s Bottom

Scrunched under the hull,
a caulking gun in one hand
and a mallet in the other,
my body holds its breath,
listening for the flooding in.
Should the sea I've wept
start knocking with its fists,
the weathered vessel of my life
would welcome it, and gently
come to shallow, then to rest
on endless, beachless shore.
Where air makes mock of water,
where whales that fed on teeming clouds
flop dry, too fat and few
for miracle to claim, O Deep,
I might have been glad.

Cadaver in a Landscape

The breastbone bobs on a sea of Latin.
The scrotum frowns in a forgotten tongue.
Toss them a ball or wicker hoop, the hands
will catch whichever before the rest
of the Resurrection knows what day it is.
Find a chimney and light a fire.
The stumpy wings of lungs will bite
the woodsmoke from the weather,
the brain too flush to tell the face
the nose is gone, the jaw left hanging
in perpetual surprise, airing two perfect
horseshoes of perfect teeth.
The knife tip they might close on's bare
but for the taste of rain and stubble fields,
of the broken ranks of apple trees,
the sharpness of a Protestant spire
rising, inquiringly, in middle distance.
The blood in the brain forgets its hemispheres,
grows round and round like the tree
lost at the edge of the woods,
rooted deep and tall as the cadaver
passes by, a promiscuity of nerves,
a handsome cranium, some feet
unbent by shoes but walking, always
walking, in search of all the man
flesh has to hold inside.

The Sunbath

Just me and the groundhogs and the dogs.
And the longhorns making water across the road
and the woodpecker tapping out a message to the future
on the leftover phone pole, and the horsefly, all teeth,
and June bugs and Junebug-munching ducks and geese
and crows, and the neighbor's colt trotting to the gate
for a sniff of my impoverished flesh, my white
underwear and tennis shoes snuggling in the clover,
strangers thrown together in the absence of the master
of the house, whose presence I know in every grapevine,
fencepost and shrub, the hot-colored rose petals
of my lids shut tight against the star we never tire of
telling ourselves must feed upon us,
indifferent and voracious in having all
it has and nothing else.

Cold Nest

I ate the stray cough drop
just to get rid of it.
I poured the hot tea
just to watch it grow cold.
Such was my love
for the outside world
I sought the puffy vinyl coat
among my closet's neat orders
of blazers and shirts.
I waited for the dove
at her cold nest
to come and tell me *dove, dove,*
her annual announcement,
meaning just that: *dove,*
never *I am* a *dove,* or even
I am *dove,* my ashen body fluffed
with information,
my house of sticks and shit
neither burgled nor broken free of.
With your first squinty glimpse of it
why ask me, then, is it nothing
not to die, to come back home
each clockwork time?
Such a question is all command
with no ear for what it asks,
a conductor calling
Papers please or *Tickets please*
or *Any proofs of travel.*

Nothing Else

Who put a feather
in the suggestion box?
Who says that I should fly?
I can sing, if nothing else,
and failing that can strut around
in heels, or carry them hooked
on the fingers of one hand,
my fluted glass in the other,
or I can let them drop,
like birds that always die in pairs
on the marble floor
of whatever palace I'm drunk in.
Have you ever eaten at the table
of the Archduke Gesa von Hapsburg?
Ask me if I have.
Have you ever heard
the despairing laugh
of the hawk, devouring
the young ones that have fallen
from her nest? It's horrible,
but breaks off beautifully,
at unexpected moments,
like the journals of M. Guillotin,
a man with huge hands
and a delicate handwriting
before becoming a machine,
his journals just now uppermost
in enlightened minds.
I sit with them all night
by the fire, staying awake
for some interruption,
a knock on the door. I jump.

My cup of pencils falls
but doesn't spill and I am grateful.
How sad does that make me?
Please, Monsieur,
Do Not Feed the People.
They've never been happier
or more hungry.

Jonah's Gourd

The fruit, the vine,
the thick leaves each
an anvil for the sun.
In the whale, so what?
But in the gourd, what seeds!
The wise men gather in clusters
to consider them.
The wise men look each other
up and down:
Have you *seen* your face this morning,
like someone's who's been sleeping
on the ground?
Jonah waits longways on a bench,
confined to his own stinging points
in time and space,
alone but for an empty paper cup
at his heels.
One sees him and thinks
of Mozart's murderers.
In what lime pits will their corpses keep?
One sees Jonah waiting there, longways
on his bench, the cup at his heels,
and remembers
everything in this world
comes either pointy and long
or hollow and round,
which is to say one is ready to confess
there is no third sex.
The wise men don't believe it.
A happy ending *is* arranged
here outside the city walls,
where Jonah never claimed

he couldn't outshine the sinner in his sin
and turn his wife over for stoning,
both in the same afternoon.
And on the dreaded Day of Judgment,
as evidence, should it be asked for,
the wise men will deliver to the bum
buckets of congratulation, fruit and flowers,
as if he'd given birth
to each and every worldly king
wearing burlap, and with an ashcan
for a throne, his Paradise consisting
of a single vine, shaking its leaves
over his head between his knees,
its plague a worm
as lonesome as himself.

Goat Shack

I sign my name to the forehead of a skull
cast in plaster, then print it neatly, then go out
and milk my goats. It's two in the morning.
You're guessing I'm one of your eccentric
gentleman farmers, but this is the city.
You're thinking my building is three-quarters
empty, and in this your thinking is exact.
That no one has taken my goats for meat
defies all explanation. Their corrugated shack
has been gone so long I hardly remember
putting it together for them, from a kit.
The night alone, electric, black, and hot,
keeps the snipers off, at least. The milk comes
with me up five flights, to the mother of a child
that hates me for it. This going out and up
and down again, it's an ancient gesture, always
threatening to explode. When they hear
my metal door groan open, the goats come alive
beneath their ceiling of stars, which will not condescend
to find the flaw in their roof and come tinkling in
like something from a book of miracles.
One night, from their milking, I very likely
won't come back, and not because I'm shot.
Whoever finds the skull in my apartment,
my name twice on it, once printed, once in script,
read the whole happy fortune of mankind.
I've never known anything of the woman but
one clean hand and half a hateful face.
Her breasts I've dreamed of, as who could not?,
a couple of graphite pencils
written right down to the nubs.

Night Job

Sir Laurence Olivier,
reduced to playing Zeus
confined to a throne,
with a beard pasted on,
was looking down on me
from the black pyramid
of an apartment block.
I was in a canoe, in the middle
of the boatlake, dumping a tv.
I held the god's gaze
without returning it, without
looking up, myself a lesser god
of earth *and* sea just barely
balanced. What splash there was
was the tv's. It was a bright
building block the lake's throat
closed over. What depth
there was to the lake lit up,
black in a flash. Zeus's lips moved
like a dog's lips ought: awfully,
in two installments, alive
beneath the beard.
At the bottom of the lake
only Zeus might shatter
the bug-eyed sleep of fish,
flash through the blackness
of such minds as fish possess,
their hearts overflowing
with admiration for the great
and famous fish of old.

Wordsworth

Below you, in the neighbor's garden,
the hives are roaring like the Keswick Rail.
Children kiss through the rungs of a chair,
some game they've carried to the logical end
of the end of the gravel path. The girl withdraws
her cheek. He laughs. Mouths in love
kiss each other to death, and those intending
to sing are stung prodigiously instead.
But here comes the beekeeper, without his veils,
dressed rather like the gentleman he is.
The children are caught in their good clothes.
The un-ghost-sheeted man turns up
his nose, disappears into his greenhouse
with the chair. The children cover their faces
with their hands. Forgetting they've come
by different roads, they go away together,
leaving the garden emptied, you make note,
but for a worker roaming up and down
the paths of broken flowers, free for a moment
of the passion of the hive, whatever wagging lust
her sting alone might hold trolling now
for the one stupid tongue that might describe it.
Where sings your brother, that *other* Wordsworth,
crooning for Rousseau as your teeth are falling out?
Regarding lovers, in one thing only you and I agree:
what makes their faces are the hands
in which they're buried.

Dawn on Grace Street

The crickets polish their bodies
on the grass.

The grass is sharp and fresh,
like nothing that wants to live forever
ever is.

On the oozy stump of a dogwood tree
an owl has planted the skull
of a mouse.

You'd think the skull is a small white stone
or a pink sea shell
put there by a child
with a castle in mind.

A thickset girl, in a satin dress,
starts puking in the grass.

A boy in half a tux
holds her small sequined bag,
with her every heave says
sorry, like a promise,
for not just letting it fall.

Book Report

On Valentine's, in the coldest month,
I took a paper knife and cut the gut
of an envelope. The envelope was the size
and approximate shape of my head,
lying on my desk like a head, and spewed
about a hundred red babies. I jumped up
proud as a phone pole, the blood
hammering in me, gilding every inner surface
with its sticky insistence, from the tops
of the pages of *1000 Places to See Before You Die*
to the indexed aliases of *The Complete Public Enemy*,
to the tingling spine of my *Big Book of Erotica*.
"Izzy the Push shot Hamburger Molly."
So said the great historians of crime.
Istanbul was someplace you could go, if you
were enthralled with the fierce desert faiths
of more innocent times. In England
they'd mount you on the parlor floor.
They'd be perfect gentlemen about it
and you'd be gorgeous as a bearskin spread
before the roaring fire. When came the inevitable
time for me to talk I tested, like Proust, every chair
in the room, considered the redness of velvet
and the straightness of backs, choosing absolutely
the reddest and straightest and, at long last,
sitting down, telling the class the story of my birth,
which I'd read about not in a book
but in some terrifying letters, a divorce decree,
and its anniversary, which I attended without fail,
and how to celebrate most recently I'd asked
my parents, each in their discrete hatefulness,
for a maze of ancient boxwood hedge,

like the one I'd seen in *The Shining*, because
I wanted to run for my life and get lost
when I wanted, and always know where I was.
"Ambitious blood you got here in Bleeding Heart."
I always wanted to say that to somebody,
in a movie, maybe, and have the audience gasp
with recognition, like I was naming
somewhere where they lived.

Late Riser

One of these days
I'll catch the world sleeping.
I'll be the only one to catch
the elms breezing by,
like it was a breeze carried them
and hardly any effort of their feet
right past our little wilderness of homes.
I'll congratulate myself,
then have to wait for the sleepyheads
in their houses to get up and ask
what the fuck happened to their trees,
and when they never do ask and never do
get up, when I explore the houses,
find the beds unslept-in, the kitchens
spotlessly clean, I'll go to the craters
still fresh in the grass, find a deep one
and crawl in, pull the dirt around me
like a velvet cape. I'll try to sleep,
but why? I'm not sleepy.
I just want more than I need
of the only blessed thing that's left.
You can meet my neighbors
if you go to Heaven.
Just look how they gobble
from empty plates and gulp
from empty cups!

Neighborhood

Here comes God, breaking elms like a cyclone
in his hands. And here sits Anne who will recall it
on the porch of her old age, a braid of white hair
looping down, turning into a toy for the cat.
A cat is something that will claw you to death
when you're trying to save its stupid life,
bundling it hissing from the boiling storm,
the hated love that smashes what it touches
and leaves untouched and trembling
the kids that burst from the toolshed,
a happy confusion of friends and hangers-on.
From a basement window: *Leave it, Anne!*
Let it go! It don't love you like you do!
We don't know if we know the girl or not.
We don't know half our own first names,
something or other with the braids and the cat.
The cat gets away. The houses blink
in shock, in sudden light, bright green.
And the cat comes back, scowling and wet,
crazy Anne crying its many-hyphened name
like some thing she thinks she used to love.

The Pedestal

for the women of East Sutton Park, County Kent

At last you must begin the lazy business of forgetting
the hog in his pen, the fox in her den,
the thrush in its crystal grief.

You must read all the Dostoyevsky in the library,
and forget it. You must read the fortunes
of a hundred fortune cookies

and defy each fate in turn. While you're at it
devour every word of Aquinas, the Speechless,
his long life of last meals, beer and buttery

lobster, and melting purple sherbet,
blood samples wagging from his fingertips
like drops eternal and intoxicating.

Out there in the un-incarcerated world
a sailor puts his spit into the sea, sings a few
sad lines about his Irish love.

No, Mother, the Earth didn't stop, but it gave
a shudder. Father, it faltered. And gentle ladies,
you know it best, the world's no place

for the steady of heart. No place to stand
before a marble pedestal, eye to eye
with the head it supports.

The Mirror

Yes, Bruce Rodgers,
God sees you masturbating.
But doesn't exactly *watch*.
He's looking for you in the mirror,
finding everything there but your face.
That's always in some *other* mirror
it can never pull itself out of.
If yours is the face God thinks it is
it'll be lost in all the mirrors
God can lose it lurking in.
Imagine the millionth hurricane,
the millionth time going to the supermarket
without glass in the plate glass front.
One reflection, Bruce.
A mirror more, my friend.
And the image of God's undone.

First Man on Earth

for Lisa Nardi

He'd only occupied a little space
in the immeasurably breathable universe
of things: the coil of twine,
the dust of yeast, the pile of stones
that would grow into the castle
where the Devil would retire
after the Diet of Worms.
Those stones, the First Man liked to tell,
were almost translucently white,
and on overcast days
the castle looked like it might
fuse itself to the ceiling of the sky.
He had had a wife,
some dim memory of children.
When he went in search of clothes for them
she gasped when he got back, dressed
as an arbor, the weird leaves
reddened to leather.
After many suchlike scenes
he walked off for no reason
they could articulate, leaving them
to wear out their ruffles,
to eat their pheasant in contentment
with three-tined forks.
He was gone so long we agreed,
without saying, that he wasn't coming back.
Very early one morning
we were all outside
in our underwear and bathrobes,
looking at a car flipped upside down,

when he walked up behind us
and asked what happened.
"Don't you ever just *die?*"
somebody said.
The possibilities in those days
were endless and stupid,
the bells in church towers
heavy as cars, balanced like buckets
of nothing over your head.
You pulled a string.
The buckets tipped,
spilled their alarums
and surprise.

Choking Baby

My first mouthful
of broken heart.
My face bunched up
in all the wrong places,
my eyes burned clean
as a pan when it screams
in cooling water.
I open and close
my humongous hands,
kneading air like earth,
earth like my parents' bodies.
I want air in my lungs
like I want walls.
I need a scream to slam its fist
into my mouth.
I have no teeth,
among other conveniences.
I have ten fingers
and ten toes.
I grab for nothing
with everything I've got.
My everything is only human,
perfected not
without the cry
of what is closed.

Selected Silences

for Chris McKenney

When the boy arrived
at the end of the day
a cricket sang its warning
and the boy ran for cover
under the singer's glossy shell.
The responding silence
of the woods and of the row
of brick apartment blocks
with lights coming on
at the edge of the woods
and of the freeway just beyond them,
dying early on a Sunday...
you can hear these in the songs
the boy will teach himself to sing,
and in these the songs
hear better what they are:
more and better silence
and a singing for the same.

Acknowledgments

Some of these poems first appeared in the following periodicals: *Bellevue Literary Review*, *Carolina Quarterly*, *Dappled Things*, *FIELD*, *Gulf Coast*, *Kenyon Review Online*, *New World Writing*, *Prairie Schooner*, *Rattle*, *South Carolina Review*, *Storyscape*, and *Third Coast*.

Warm thanks to the teachers and friends who gave their support and good counsel throughout the writing of these poems: Lisa Nardi, Carolyn White, Rita Felski, Jim and Barbara Peters, Bo Millner, Kristen Taylor-Martin, Astor and Gino Defulgentiis, Jean Roy Jones, Mary Ruefle, David Wojahn, Ralph Angel, Clare Rossini, and Gregory Orr. Thanks especially to my partner, David Fletcher.

The FIELD Poetry Series

1993   Dennis Schmitz, *About Night: Selected and New Poems*
        Marianne Boruch, *Moss Burning*

1994   Russell Edson, *The Tunnel: Selected Poems*

1996   Killarney Clary, *By Common Salt*

1997   Marianne Boruch, *A Stick That Breaks and Breaks*

1998   Jon Loomis, *Vanitas Motel*
        Franz Wright, *Ill Lit: Selected & New Poems*

1999   Marcia Southwick, *A Saturday Night at the Flying Dog and Other Poems*

2000   Timothy Kelly, *Stronger*

2001   Ralph Burns, *Ghost Notes*
        Jon Loomis, *The Pleasure Principle*

2002   Angie Estes, *Voice-Over*
        Tom Andrews, *Random Symmetries: The Collected Poems of Tom Andrews*

2003   Carol Moldaw, *The Lightning Field*

2004   Marianne Boruch, *Poems: New & Selected*
        Jonah Winter, *Amnesia*

2005   Angie Estes, *Chez Nous*
        Beckian Fritz Goldberg, *Lie Awake Lake*

2006   Jean Gallagher, *Stubborn*

2007   Mary Cornish, *Red Studio*

2008   J. W. Marshall, *Meaning a Cloud*
        Timothy Kelly, *The Extremities*

2009   Dennis Hinrichsen, *Kurosawa's Dog*
        Angie Estes, *Tryst*

2010   Amy Newlove Schroeder, *The Sleep Hotel*

2011   Timothy O'Keefe, *The Goodbye Town*

2012   Jean Gallagher, *Start*
        Mark Neely, *Beasts of the Hill*

2013   Mary Ann Samyn, *My Life in Heaven*
        Beckian Fritz Goldberg, *Egypt from Space*
        Angie Estes, *Enchantée*